PASTORAL RECORD

THE LIFE MINISTRY OF

_____

Note it in a book, that it may be
for the time to come.—*Isa. 30:8*

Prepared by
J. N. GREENE

Abingdon Press
NASHVILLE

ICN 301416

CONTENTS

RECORD OF PASTORATES

DATE BEGAN	CHURCH	ADDRESS	HOW ASSIGNED TO PASTORATE	MEMBER-SHIP	SALARY

RECORD OF BAPTISMS

DATE	NAME	ADDRESS	PLACE	AGE	REMARKS

RECORD OF BAPTISMS

DATE	NAME	ADDRESS	PLACE	AGE	REMARKS

RECORD OF BAPTISMS

DATE	NAME	ADDRESS	PLACE	AGE	REMARKS

RECORD OF BAPTISMS

DATE	NAME	ADDRESS	PLACE	AGE	REMARKS

RECORD OF BAPTISMS

DATE	NAME	ADDRESS	PLACE	AGE	REMARKS

RECORD OF BAPTISMS

DATE	NAME	ADDRESS	PLACE	AGE	REMARKS

RECORD OF BAPTISMS

DATE	NAME	ADDRESS	PLACE	AGE	REMARKS

RECORD OF BAPTISMS

DATE	NAME	ADDRESS	PLACE	AGE	REMARKS

RECORD OF BAPTISMS

DATE	NAME	ADDRESS	PLACE	AGE	REMARKS

RECORD OF BAPTISMS

DATE	NAME	ADDRESS	PLACE	AGE	REMARKS

RECORD OF BAPTISMS

DATE	NAME	ADDRESS	PLACE	AGE	REMARKS

RECORD OF BAPTISMS

DATE	NAME	ADDRESS	PLACE	AGE	REMARKS

RECORD OF BAPTISMS

DATE	NAME	ADDRESS	PLACE	AGE	REMARKS

RECORD OF BAPTISMS

DATE	NAME	ADDRESS	PLACE	AGE	REMARKS

RECORD OF BAPTISMS

DATE	NAME	ADDRESS	PLACE	AGE	REMARKS

RECORD OF BAPTISMS

DATE	NAME	ADDRESS	PLACE	AGE	REMARKS

RECORD OF BAPTISMS

DATE	NAME	ADDRESS	PLACE	AGE	REMARKS

RECORD OF BAPTISMS

DATE	NAME	ADDRESS	PLACE	AGE	REMARKS

RECORD OF BAPTISMS

DATE	NAME	ADDRESS	PLACE	AGE	REMARKS

RECORD OF BAPTISMS

DATE	NAME	ADDRESS	PLACE	AGE	REMARKS

RECORD OF BAPTISMS

DATE	NAME	ADDRESS	PLACE	AGE	REMARKS

RECORD OF BAPTISMS

DATE	NAME	ADDRESS	PLACE	AGE	REMARKS

RECORD OF BAPTISMS

DATE	NAME	ADDRESS	PLACE	AGE	REMARKS

RECORD OF BAPTISMS

DATE	NAME	ADDRESS	PLACE	AGE	REMARKS

RECORD OF BAPTISMS

DATE	NAME	ADDRESS	PLACE	AGE	REMARKS

RECORD OF BAPTISMS

DATE	NAME	ADDRESS	PLACE	AGE	REMARKS

RECORD OF BAPTISMS

DATE	NAME	ADDRESS	PLACE	AGE	REMARKS

RECORD OF BAPTISMS

DATE	NAME	ADDRESS	PLACE	AGE	REMARKS

RECORD OF BAPTISMS

DATE	NAME	ADDRESS	PLACE	AGE	REMARKS

RECORD OF BAPTISMS

DATE	NAME	ADDRESS	PLACE	AGE	REMARKS

RECORD OF BAPTISMS

DATE	NAME	ADDRESS	PLACE	AGE	REMARKS

RECORD OF BAPTISMS

DATE	NAME	ADDRESS	PLACE	AGE	REMARKS

RECORD OF BAPTISMS

DATE	NAME	ADDRESS	PLACE	AGE	REMARKS

RECORD OF BAPTISMS

DATE	NAME	ADDRESS	PLACE	AGE	REMARKS

RECORD OF BAPTISMS

DATE	NAME	ADDRESS	PLACE	AGE	REMARKS

RECORD OF BAPTISMS

DATE	NAME	ADDRESS	PLACE	AGE	REMARKS

RECORD OF BAPTISMS

DATE	NAME	ADDRESS	PLACE	AGE	REMARKS

RECORD OF BAPTISMS

DATE	NAME	ADDRESS	PLACE	AGE	REMARKS

RECORD OF BAPTISMS

DATE	NAME	ADDRESS	PLACE	AGE	REMARKS

RECORD OF BAPTISMS

DATE	NAME	ADDRESS	PLACE	AGE	REMARKS

RECORD OF BAPTISMS

DATE	NAME	ADDRESS	PLACE	AGE	REMARKS

RECORD OF BAPTISMS

DATE	NAME	ADDRESS	PLACE	AGE	REMARKS

RECORD OF BAPTISMS

DATE	NAME	ADDRESS	PLACE	AGE	REMARKS

RECORD OF BAPTISMS

DATE	NAME	ADDRESS	PLACE	AGE	REMARKS

RECORD OF MEMBERS RECEIVED OR CONFIRMED

DATE	NAME	ADDRESS	SINGLE MARRIED WIDOWED	AGE	REMARKS

RECORD OF MEMBERS RECEIVED OR CONFIRMED

DATE	NAME	ADDRESS	SINGLE MARRIED WIDOWED	AGE	REMARKS

RECORD OF MEMBERS RECEIVED OR CONFIRMED

DATE	NAME	ADDRESS	SINGLE MARRIED WIDOWED	AGE	REMARKS

RECORD OF MEMBERS RECEIVED OR CONFIRMED

DATE	NAME	ADDRESS	SINGLE MARRIED WIDOWED	AGE	REMARKS

RECORD OF MEMBERS RECEIVED OR CONFIRMED

DATE	NAME	ADDRESS	SINGLE MARRIED WIDOWED	AGE	REMARKS

RECORD OF MEMBERS RECEIVED OR CONFIRMED

DATE	NAME	ADDRESS	SINGLE MARRIED WIDOWED	AGE	REMARKS

RECORD OF MEMBERS RECEIVED OR CONFIRMED

DATE	NAME	ADDRESS	SINGLE MARRIED WIDOWED	AGE	REMARKS

RECORD OF MEMBERS RECEIVED OR CONFIRMED

DATE	NAME	ADDRESS	SINGLE MARRIED WIDOWED	AGE	REMARKS

RECORD OF MEMBERS RECEIVED OR CONFIRMED

DATE	NAME	ADDRESS	SINGLE MARRIED WIDOWED	AGE	REMARKS

RECORD OF MEMBERS RECEIVED OR CONFIRMED

DATE	NAME	ADDRESS	SINGLE MARRIED WIDOWED	AGE	REMARKS

RECORD OF MEMBERS RECEIVED OR CONFIRMED

DATE	NAME	ADDRESS	SINGLE MARRIED WIDOWED	AGE	REMARKS

RECORD OF MEMBERS RECEIVED OR CONFIRMED

DATE	NAME	ADDRESS	SINGLE MARRIED WIDOWED	AGE	REMARKS

RECORD OF MEMBERS RECEIVED OR CONFIRMED

DATE	NAME	ADDRESS	SINGLE MARRIED WIDOWED	AGE	REMARKS

RECORD OF MEMBERS RECEIVED OR CONFIRMED

DATE	NAME	ADDRESS	SINGLE MARRIED WIDOWED	AGE	REMARKS

RECORD OF MEMBERS RECEIVED OR CONFIRMED

DATE	NAME	ADDRESS	SINGLE MARRIED WIDOWED	AGE	REMARKS

RECORD OF MEMBERS RECEIVED OR CONFIRMED

DATE	NAME	ADDRESS	SINGLE MARRIED WIDOWED	AGE	REMARKS

RECORD OF MEMBERS RECEIVED OR CONFIRMED

DATE	NAME	ADDRESS	SINGLE MARRIED WIDOWED	AGE	REMARKS

RECORD OF MEMBERS RECEIVED OR CONFIRMED

DATE	NAME	ADDRESS	SINGLE MARRIED WIDOWED	AGE	REMARKS

RECORD OF MEMBERS RECEIVED OR CONFIRMED

DATE	NAME	ADDRESS	SINGLE MARRIED WIDOWED	AGE	REMARKS

RECORD OF MEMBERS RECEIVED OR CONFIRMED

DATE	NAME	ADDRESS	SINGLE MARRIED WIDOWED	AGE	REMARKS

RECORD OF MEMBERS RECEIVED OR CONFIRMED

DATE	NAME	ADDRESS	SINGLE MARRIED WIDOWED	AGE	REMARKS

RECORD OF MEMBERS RECEIVED OR CONFIRMED

DATE	NAME	ADDRESS	SINGLE MARRIED WIDOWED	AGE	REMARKS

RECORD OF MEMBERS RECEIVED OR CONFIRMED

DATE	NAME	ADDRESS	SINGLE MARRIED WIDOWED	AGE	REMARKS

RECORD OF MEMBERS RECEIVED OR CONFIRMED

DATE	NAME	ADDRESS	SINGLE MARRIED WIDOWED	AGE	REMARKS

RECORD OF MEMBERS RECEIVED OR CONFIRMED

DATE	NAME	ADDRESS	SINGLE MARRIED WIDOWED	AGE	REMARKS

RECORD OF MEMBERS RECEIVED OR CONFIRMED

DATE	NAME	ADDRESS	SINGLE MARRIED WIDOWED	AGE	REMARKS

RECORD OF MEMBERS RECEIVED OR CONFIRMED

DATE	NAME	ADDRESS	SINGLE MARRIED WIDOWED	AGE	REMARKS

RECORD OF MEMBERS RECEIVED OR CONFIRMED

DATE	NAME	ADDRESS	SINGLE MARRIED WIDOWED	AGE	REMARKS

RECORD OF MEMBERS RECEIVED OR CONFIRMED

DATE	NAME	ADDRESS	SINGLE MARRIED WIDOWED	AGE	REMARKS

RECORD OF MEMBERS RECEIVED OR CONFIRMED

DATE	NAME	ADDRESS	SINGLE MARRIED WIDOWED	AGE	REMARKS

RECORD OF MEMBERS RECEIVED OR CONFIRMED

DATE	NAME	ADDRESS	SINGLE MARRIED WIDOWED	AGE	REMARKS

RECORD OF MEMBERS RECEIVED OR CONFIRMED

DATE	NAME	ADDRESS	SINGLE MARRIED WIDOWED	AGE	REMARKS

RECORD OF MEMBERS RECEIVED OR CONFIRMED

DATE	NAME	ADDRESS	SINGLE MARRIED WIDOWED	AGE	REMARKS

RECORD OF MEMBERS RECEIVED OR CONFIRMED

DATE	NAME	ADDRESS	SINGLE MARRIED WIDOWED	AGE	REMARKS

RECORD OF MEMBERS RECEIVED OR CONFIRMED

DATE	NAME	ADDRESS	SINGLE MARRIED WIDOWED	AGE	REMARKS

RECORD OF MEMBERS RECEIVED OR CONFIRMED

DATE	NAME	ADDRESS	SINGLE MARRIED WIDOWED	AGE	REMARKS

RECORD OF MEMBERS RECEIVED OR CONFIRMED

DATE	NAME	ADDRESS	SINGLE MARRIED WIDOWED	AGE	REMARKS

RECORD OF MEMBERS RECEIVED OR CONFIRMED

DATE	NAME	ADDRESS	SINGLE MARRIED WIDOWED	AGE	REMARKS

RECORD OF MEMBERS RECEIVED OR CONFIRMED

DATE	NAME	ADDRESS	SINGLE MARRIED WIDOWED	AGE	REMARKS

RECORD OF MEMBERS RECEIVED OR CONFIRMED

DATE	NAME	ADDRESS	SINGLE MARRIED WIDOWED	AGE	REMARKS

RECORD OF MEMBERS RECEIVED OR CONFIRMED

DATE	NAME	ADDRESS	SINGLE MARRIED WIDOWED	AGE	REMARKS

RECORD OF MEMBERS RECEIVED OR CONFIRMED

DATE	NAME	ADDRESS	SINGLE MARRIED WIDOWED	AGE	REMARKS

RECORD OF MEMBERS RECEIVED OR CONFIRMED

DATE	NAME	ADDRESS	SINGLE MARRIED WIDOWED	AGE	REMARKS

RECORD OF MEMBERS RECEIVED OR CONFIRMED

DATE	NAME	ADDRESS	SINGLE MARRIED WIDOWED	AGE	REMARKS

RECORD OF MARRIAGES

DATE	NAMES	ADDRESSES	AGES	OCCUPATION	FEE	PLACE OF CEREMONY

RECORD OF MARRIAGES

DATE	NAMES	ADDRESSES	AGES	OCCUPATION	FEE	PLACE OF CEREMONY

RECORD OF MARRIAGES

DATE	NAMES	ADDRESSES	AGES	OCCUPATION	FEE	PLACE OF CEREMONY

RECORD OF MARRIAGES

DATE	NAMES	ADDRESSES	AGES	OCCUPATION	FEE	PLACE OF CEREMONY

RECORD OF MARRIAGES

DATE	NAMES	ADDRESSES	AGES	OCCUPATION	FEE	PLACE OF CEREMONY

RECORD OF MARRIAGES

DATE	NAMES	ADDRESSES	AGES	OCCUPATION	FEE	PLACE OF CEREMONY

RECORD OF MARRIAGES

DATE	NAMES	ADDRESSES	AGES	OCCUPATION	FEE	PLACE OF CEREMONY

RECORD OF MARRIAGES

DATE	NAMES	ADDRESSES	AGES	OCCUPATION	FEE	PLACE OF CEREMONY

RECORD OF MARRIAGES

DATE	NAMES	ADDRESSES	AGES	OCCUPATION	FEE	PLACE OF CEREMONY

RECORD OF MARRIAGES

DATE	NAMES	ADDRESSES	AGES	OCCUPATION	FEE	PLACE OF CEREMONY

RECORD OF MARRIAGES

DATE	NAMES	ADDRESSES	AGES	OCCUPATION	FEE	PLACE OF CEREMONY

RECORD OF MARRIAGES

DATE	NAMES	ADDRESSES	AGES	OCCUPATION	FEE	PLACE OF CEREMONY

RECORD OF MARRIAGES

DATE	NAMES	ADDRESSES	AGES	OCCUPATION	FEE	PLACE OF CEREMONY

RECORD OF MARRIAGES

DATE	NAMES	ADDRESSES	AGES	OCCUPATION	FEE	PLACE OF CEREMONY

RECORD OF MARRIAGES

DATE	NAMES	ADDRESSES	AGES	OCCUPATION	FEE	PLACE OF CEREMONY

RECORD OF MARRIAGES

DATE	NAMES	ADDRESSES	AGES	OCCUPATION	FEE	PLACE OF CEREMONY

RECORD OF MARRIAGES

DATE	NAMES	ADDRESSES	AGES	OCCUPATION	FEE	PLACE OF CEREMONY

RECORD OF MARRIAGES

DATE	NAMES	ADDRESSES	AGES	OCCUPATION	FEE	PLACE OF CEREMONY

RECORD OF MARRIAGES

DATE	NAMES	ADDRESSES	AGES	OCCUPATION	FEE	PLACE OF CEREMONY

RECORD OF MARRIAGES

DATE	NAMES	ADDRESSES	AGES	OCCUPATION	FEE	PLACE OF CEREMONY

RECORD OF MARRIAGES

DATE	NAMES	ADDRESSES	AGES	OCCUPATION	FEE	PLACE OF CEREMONY

RECORD OF MARRIAGES

DATE	NAMES	ADDRESSES	AGES	OCCUPATION	FEE	PLACE OF CEREMONY

RECORD OF MARRIAGES

DATE	NAMES	ADDRESSES	AGES	OCCUPATION	FEE	PLACE OF CEREMONY

RECORD OF MARRIAGES

DATE	NAMES	ADDRESSES	AGES	OCCUPATION	FEE	PLACE OF CEREMONY

RECORD OF MARRIAGES

DATE	NAMES	ADDRESSES	AGES	OCCUPATION	FEE	PLACE OF CEREMONY

RECORD OF MARRIAGES

DATE	NAMES	ADDRESSES	AGES	OCCUPATION	FEE	PLACE OF CEREMONY

RECORD OF MARRIAGES

DATE	NAMES	ADDRESSES	AGES	OCCUPATION	FEE	PLACE OF CEREMONY

RECORD OF MARRIAGES

DATE	NAMES	ADDRESSES	AGES	OCCUPATION	FEE	PLACE OF CEREMONY

RECORD OF MARRIAGES

DATE	NAMES	ADDRESSES	AGES	OCCUPATION	FEE	PLACE OF CEREMONY

RECORD OF MARRIAGES

DATE	NAMES	ADDRESSES	AGES	OCCUPATION	FEE	PLACE OF CEREMONY

RECORD OF MARRIAGES

DATE	NAMES	ADDRESSES	AGES	OCCUPATION	FEE	PLACE OF CEREMONY

RECORD OF MARRIAGES

DATE	NAMES	ADDRESSES	AGES	OCCUPATION	FEE	PLACE OF CEREMONY

RECORD OF MARRIAGES

DATE	NAMES	ADDRESSES	AGES	OCCUPATION	FEE	PLACE OF CEREMONY

RECORD OF MARRIAGES

DATE	NAMES	ADDRESSES	AGES	OCCUPATION	FEE	PLACE OF CEREMONY

RECORD OF MARRIAGES

DATE	NAMES	ADDRESSES	AGES	OCCUPATION	FEE	PLACE OF CEREMONY

RECORD OF MARRIAGES

DATE	NAMES	ADDRESSES	AGES	OCCUPATION	FEE	PLACE OF CEREMONY

RECORD OF MARRIAGES

DATE	NAMES	ADDRESSES	AGES	OCCUPATION	FEE	PLACE OF CEREMONY

RECORD OF MARRIAGES

DATE	NAMES	ADDRESSES	AGES	OCCUPATION	FEE	PLACE OF CEREMONY

RECORD OF MARRIAGES

DATE	NAMES	ADDRESSES	AGES	OCCUPATION	FEE	PLACE OF CEREMONY

RECORD OF MARRIAGES

DATE	NAMES	ADDRESSES	AGES	OCCUPATION	FEE	PLACE OF CEREMONY

RECORD OF MARRIAGES

DATE	NAMES	ADDRESSES	AGES	OCCUPATION	FEE	PLACE OF CEREMONY

RECORD OF MARRIAGES

DATE	NAMES	ADDRESSES	AGES	OCCUPATION	FEE	PLACE OF CEREMONY

RECORD OF MARRIAGES

DATE	NAMES	ADDRESSES	AGES	OCCUPATION	FEE	PLACE OF CEREMONY

RECORD OF MARRIAGES

DATE	NAMES	ADDRESSES	AGES	OCCUPATION	FEE	PLACE OF CEREMONY

RECORD OF MARRIAGES

DATE	NAMES	ADDRESSES	AGES	OCCUPATION	FEE	PLACE OF CEREMONY

RECORD OF MARRIAGES

DATE	NAMES	ADDRESSES	AGES	OCCUPATION	FEE	PLACE OF CEREMONY

RECORD OF MARRIAGES

DATE	NAMES	ADDRESSES	AGES	OCCUPATION	FEE	PLACE OF CEREMONY

RECORD OF MARRIAGES

DATE	NAMES	ADDRESSES	AGES	OCCUPATION	FEE	PLACE OF CEREMONY

RECORD OF MARRIAGES

DATE	NAMES	ADDRESSES	AGES	OCCUPATION	FEE	PLACE OF CEREMONY

RECORD OF FUNERALS

DATE	NAME	ADDRESS	AGE	TEXT OR SUBJECT	CHURCH MEMBER?	WHERE HELD

RECORD OF FUNERALS

DATE	NAME	ADDRESS	AGE	TEXT OR SUBJECT	CHURCH MEMBER?	WHERE HELD

RECORD OF FUNERALS

DATE	NAME	ADDRESS	AGE	TEXT OR SUBJECT	CHURCH MEMBER?	WHERE HELD

RECORD OF FUNERALS

DATE	NAME	ADDRESS	AGE	TEXT OR SUBJECT	CHURCH MEMBER?	WHERE HELD

RECORD OF FUNERALS

DATE	NAME	ADDRESS	AGE	TEXT OR SUBJECT	CHURCH MEMBER?	WHERE HELD

RECORD OF FUNERALS

DATE	NAME	ADDRESS	AGE	TEXT OR SUBJECT	CHURCH MEMBER?	WHERE HELD

RECORD OF FUNERALS

DATE	NAME	ADDRESS	AGE	TEXT OR SUBJECT	CHURCH MEMBER?	WHERE HELD

RECORD OF FUNERALS

DATE	NAME	ADDRESS	AGE	TEXT OR SUBJECT	CHURCH MEMBER?	WHERE HELD

RECORD OF FUNERALS

DATE	NAME	ADDRESS	AGE	TEXT OR SUBJECT	CHURCH MEMBER?	WHERE HELD

RECORD OF FUNERALS

DATE	NAME	ADDRESS	AGE	TEXT OR SUBJECT	CHURCH MEMBER?	WHERE HELD

RECORD OF FUNERALS

DATE	NAME	ADDRESS	AGE	TEXT OR SUBJECT	CHURCH MEMBER?	WHERE HELD

RECORD OF FUNERALS

DATE	NAME	ADDRESS	AGE	TEXT OR SUBJECT	CHURCH MEMBER?	WHERE HELD

RECORD OF FUNERALS

DATE	NAME	ADDRESS	AGE	TEXT OR SUBJECT	CHURCH MEMBER?	WHERE HELD

RECORD OF FUNERALS

DATE	NAME	ADDRESS	AGE	TEXT OR SUBJECT	CHURCH MEMBER?	WHERE HELD

RECORD OF FUNERALS

DATE	NAME	ADDRESS	AGE	TEXT OR SUBJECT	CHURCH MEMBER?	WHERE HELD

RECORD OF FUNERALS

DATE	NAME	ADDRESS	AGE	TEXT OR SUBJECT	CHURCH MEMBER?	WHERE HELD

RECORD OF FUNERALS

DATE	NAME	ADDRESS	AGE	TEXT OR SUBJECT	CHURCH MEMBER?	WHERE HELD

RECORD OF FUNERALS

DATE	NAME	ADDRESS	AGE	TEXT OR SUBJECT	CHURCH MEMBER?	WHERE HELD

RECORD OF FUNERALS

DATE	NAME	ADDRESS	AGE	TEXT OR SUBJECT	CHURCH MEMBER?	WHERE HELD

RECORD OF FUNERALS

DATE	NAME	ADDRESS	AGE	TEXT OR SUBJECT	CHURCH MEMBER?	WHERE HELD

RECORD OF FUNERALS

DATE	NAME	ADDRESS	AGE	TEXT OR SUBJECT	CHURCH MEMBER?	WHERE HELD

RECORD OF FUNERALS

DATE	NAME	ADDRESS	AGE	TEXT OR SUBJECT	CHURCH MEMBER?	WHERE HELD

RECORD OF FUNERALS

DATE	NAME	ADDRESS	AGE	TEXT OR SUBJECT	CHURCH MEMBER?	WHERE HELD

RECORD OF FUNERALS

DATE	NAME	ADDRESS	AGE	TEXT OR SUBJECT	CHURCH MEMBER?	WHERE HELD

RECORD OF FUNERALS

DATE	NAME	ADDRESS	AGE	TEXT OR SUBJECT	CHURCH MEMBER?	WHERE HELD

RECORD OF FUNERALS

DATE	NAME	ADDRESS	AGE	TEXT OR SUBJECT	CHURCH MEMBER?	WHERE HELD

RECORD OF FUNERALS

DATE	NAME	ADDRESS	AGE	TEXT OR SUBJECT	CHURCH MEMBER?	WHERE HELD

RECORD OF FUNERALS

DATE	NAME	ADDRESS	AGE	TEXT OR SUBJECT	CHURCH MEMBER?	WHERE HELD

RECORD OF FUNERALS

DATE	NAME	ADDRESS	AGE	TEXT OR SUBJECT	CHURCH MEMBER?	WHERE HELD

RECORD OF FUNERALS

DATE	NAME	ADDRESS	AGE	TEXT OR SUBJECT	CHURCH MEMBER?	WHERE HELD

RECORD OF FUNERALS

DATE	NAME	ADDRESS	AGE	TEXT OR SUBJECT	CHURCH MEMBER?	WHERE HELD

RECORD OF FUNERALS

DATE	NAME	ADDRESS	AGE	TEXT OR SUBJECT	CHURCH MEMBER?	WHERE HELD

RECORD OF FUNERALS

DATE	NAME	ADDRESS	AGE	TEXT OR SUBJECT	CHURCH MEMBER?	WHERE HELD

RECORD OF FUNERALS

DATE	NAME	ADDRESS	AGE	TEXT OR SUBJECT	CHURCH MEMBER?	WHERE HELD

RECORD OF FUNERALS

DATE	NAME	ADDRESS	AGE	TEXT OR SUBJECT	CHURCH MEMBER?	WHERE HELD

RECORD OF FUNERALS

DATE	NAME	ADDRESS	AGE	TEXT OR SUBJECT	CHURCH MEMBER?	WHERE HELD

RECORD OF FUNERALS

DATE	NAME	ADDRESS	AGE	TEXT OR SUBJECT	CHURCH MEMBER?	WHERE HELD

RECORD OF FUNERALS

DATE	NAME	ADDRESS	AGE	TEXT OR SUBJECT	CHURCH MEMBER?	WHERE HELD

RECORD OF FUNERALS

DATE	NAME	ADDRESS	AGE	TEXT OR SUBJECT	CHURCH MEMBER?	WHERE HELD

RECORD OF FUNERALS

DATE	NAME	ADDRESS	AGE	TEXT OR SUBJECT	CHURCH MEMBER?	WHERE HELD

RECORD OF FUNERALS

DATE	NAME	ADDRESS	AGE	TEXT OR SUBJECT	CHURCH MEMBER?	WHERE HELD

RECORD OF FUNERALS

DATE	NAME	ADDRESS	AGE	TEXT OR SUBJECT	CHURCH MEMBER?	WHERE HELD

RECORD OF FUNERALS

DATE	NAME	ADDRESS	AGE	TEXT OR SUBJECT	CHURCH MEMBER?	WHERE HELD

RECORD OF SERMONS DELIVERED

DATE	SUBJECT	TEXT	PLACE DELIVERED	REMARKS

RECORD OF SERMONS DELIVERED

DATE	SUBJECT	TEXT	PLACE DELIVERED	REMARKS

RECORD OF SERMONS DELIVERED

DATE	SUBJECT	TEXT	PLACE DELIVERED	REMARKS

RECORD OF SERMONS DELIVERED

DATE	SUBJECT	TEXT	PLACE DELIVERED	REMARKS

RECORD OF SERMONS DELIVERED

DATE	SUBJECT	TEXT	PLACE DELIVERED	REMARKS

RECORD OF SERMONS DELIVERED

DATE	SUBJECT	TEXT	PLACE DELIVERED	REMARKS

RECORD OF SERMONS DELIVERED

DATE	SUBJECT	TEXT	PLACE DELIVERED	REMARKS

RECORD OF SERMONS DELIVERED

DATE	SUBJECT	TEXT	PLACE DELIVERED	REMARKS

RECORD OF SERMONS DELIVERED

DATE	SUBJECT	TEXT	PLACE DELIVERED	REMARKS

RECORD OF SERMONS DELIVERED

DATE	SUBJECT	TEXT	PLACE DELIVERED	REMARKS

RECORD OF SERMONS DELIVERED

DATE	SUBJECT	TEXT	PLACE DELIVERED	REMARKS

RECORD OF SERMONS DELIVERED

DATE	SUBJECT	TEXT	PLACE DELIVERED	REMARKS

RECORD OF SERMONS DELIVERED

DATE	SUBJECT	TEXT	PLACE DELIVERED	REMARKS

RECORD OF SERMONS DELIVERED

DATE	SUBJECT	TEXT	PLACE DELIVERED	REMARKS

RECORD OF SERMONS DELIVERED

DATE	SUBJECT	TEXT	PLACE DELIVERED	REMARKS

RECORD OF SERMONS DELIVERED

DATE	SUBJECT	TEXT	PLACE DELIVERED	REMARKS

RECORD OF SERMONS DELIVERED

DATE	SUBJECT	TEXT	PLACE DELIVERED	REMARKS

RECORD OF SERMONS DELIVERED

DATE	SUBJECT	TEXT	PLACE DELIVERED	REMARKS

RECORD OF SERMONS DELIVERED

DATE	SUBJECT	TEXT	PLACE DELIVERED	REMARKS

RECORD OF SERMONS DELIVERED

DATE	SUBJECT	TEXT	PLACE DELIVERED	REMARKS

RECORD OF SERMONS DELIVERED

DATE	SUBJECT	TEXT	PLACE DELIVERED	REMARKS

RECORD OF SERMONS DELIVERED

DATE	SUBJECT	TEXT	PLACE DELIVERED	REMARKS

RECORD OF SERMONS DELIVERED

DATE	SUBJECT	TEXT	PLACE DELIVERED	REMARKS

RECORD OF SERMONS DELIVERED

DATE	SUBJECT	TEXT	PLACE DELIVERED	REMARKS

RECORD OF SERMONS DELIVERED

DATE	SUBJECT	TEXT	PLACE DELIVERED	REMARKS

RECORD OF SERMONS DELIVERED

DATE	SUBJECT	TEXT	PLACE DELIVERED	REMARKS

RECORD OF SERMONS DELIVERED

DATE	SUBJECT	TEXT	PLACE DELIVERED	REMARKS

RECORD OF SERMONS DELIVERED

DATE	SUBJECT	TEXT	PLACE DELIVERED	REMARKS

RECORD OF SERMONS DELIVERED

DATE	SUBJECT	TEXT	PLACE DELIVERED	REMARKS

RECORD OF SERMONS DELIVERED

DATE	SUBJECT	TEXT	PLACE DELIVERED	REMARKS

RECORD OF SERMONS DELIVERED

DATE	SUBJECT	TEXT	PLACE DELIVERED	REMARKS

RECORD OF SERMONS DELIVERED

DATE	SUBJECT	TEXT	PLACE DELIVERED	REMARKS

RECORD OF SERMONS DELIVERED

DATE	SUBJECT	TEXT	PLACE DELIVERED	REMARKS

RECORD OF SERMONS DELIVERED

DATE	SUBJECT	TEXT	PLACE DELIVERED	REMARKS

RECORD OF SERMONS DELIVERED

DATE	SUBJECT	TEXT	PLACE DELIVERED	REMARKS

RECORD OF SERMONS DELIVERED

DATE	SUBJECT	TEXT	PLACE DELIVERED	REMARKS

RECORD OF SERMONS DELIVERED

DATE	SUBJECT	TEXT	PLACE DELIVERED	REMARKS

RECORD OF SERMONS DELIVERED

DATE	SUBJECT	TEXT	PLACE DELIVERED	REMARKS

RECORD OF SERMONS DELIVERED

DATE	SUBJECT	TEXT	PLACE DELIVERED	REMARKS

RECORD OF SERMONS DELIVERED

DATE	SUBJECT	TEXT	PLACE DELIVERED	REMARKS

RECORD OF SERMONS DELIVERED

DATE	SUBJECT	TEXT	PLACE DELIVERED	REMARKS

RECORD OF SERMONS DELIVERED

DATE	SUBJECT	TEXT	PLACE DELIVERED	REMARKS

RECORD OF SERMONS DELIVERED

DATE	SUBJECT	TEXT	PLACE DELIVERED	REMARKS

RECORD OF SERMONS DELIVERED

DATE	SUBJECT	TEXT	PLACE DELIVERED	REMARKS

RECORD OF SERMONS DELIVERED

DATE	SUBJECT	TEXT	PLACE DELIVERED	REMARKS

RECORD OF SERMONS DELIVERED

DATE	SUBJECT	TEXT	PLACE DELIVERED	REMARKS

RECORD OF SERMONS DELIVERED

DATE	SUBJECT	TEXT	PLACE DELIVERED	REMARKS

RECORD OF SERMONS DELIVERED

DATE	SUBJECT	TEXT	PLACE DELIVERED	REMARKS

RECORD OF SERMONS DELIVERED

DATE	SUBJECT	TEXT	PLACE DELIVERED	REMARKS

RECORD OF SERMONS DELIVERED

DATE	SUBJECT	TEXT	PLACE DELIVERED	REMARKS

RECORD OF SERMONS DELIVERED

DATE	SUBJECT	TEXT	PLACE DELIVERED	REMARKS

RECORD OF SERMONS DELIVERED

DATE	SUBJECT	TEXT	PLACE DELIVERED	REMARKS

RECORD OF SERMONS DELIVERED

DATE	SUBJECT	TEXT	PLACE DELIVERED	REMARKS

RECORD OF SERMONS DELIVERED

DATE	SUBJECT	TEXT	PLACE DELIVERED	REMARKS

RECORD OF SERMONS DELIVERED

DATE	SUBJECT	TEXT	PLACE DELIVERED	REMARKS

RECORD OF SERMONS DELIVERED

DATE	SUBJECT	TEXT	PLACE DELIVERED	REMARKS

RECORD OF SERMONS DELIVERED

DATE	SUBJECT	TEXT	PLACE DELIVERED	REMARKS

RECORD OF SERMONS DELIVERED

DATE	SUBJECT	TEXT	PLACE DELIVERED	REMARKS

RECORD OF SERMONS DELIVERED

DATE	SUBJECT	TEXT	PLACE DELIVERED	REMARKS

RECORD OF SERMONS DELIVERED

DATE	SUBJECT	TEXT	PLACE DELIVERED	REMARKS

RECORD OF SERMONS DELIVERED

DATE	SUBJECT	TEXT	PLACE DELIVERED	REMARKS

RECORD OF SERMONS DELIVERED

DATE	SUBJECT	TEXT	PLACE DELIVERED	REMARKS

RECORD OF SERMONS DELIVERED

DATE	SUBJECT	TEXT	PLACE DELIVERED	REMARKS

RECORD OF SERMONS DELIVERED

DATE	SUBJECT	TEXT	PLACE DELIVERED	REMARKS

RECORD OF SERMONS DELIVERED

DATE	SUBJECT	TEXT	PLACE DELIVERED	REMARKS

RECORD OF SERMONS DELIVERED

DATE	SUBJECT	TEXT	PLACE DELIVERED	REMARKS

RECORD OF SERMONS DELIVERED

DATE	SUBJECT	TEXT	PLACE DELIVERED	REMARKS

RECORD OF SERMONS DELIVERED

DATE	SUBJECT	TEXT	PLACE DELIVERED	REMARKS

RECORD OF SERMONS DELIVERED

DATE	SUBJECT	TEXT	PLACE DELIVERED	REMARKS

RECORD OF SERMONS DELIVERED

DATE	SUBJECT	TEXT	PLACE DELIVERED	REMARKS

RECORD OF SERMONS DELIVERED

DATE	SUBJECT	TEXT	PLACE DELIVERED	REMARKS

RECORD OF SERMONS DELIVERED

DATE	SUBJECT	TEXT	PLACE DELIVERED	REMARKS

RECORD OF SERMONS DELIVERED

DATE	SUBJECT	TEXT	PLACE DELIVERED	REMARKS

RECORD OF SERMONS DELIVERED

DATE	SUBJECT	TEXT	PLACE DELIVERED	REMARKS

RECORD OF SERMONS DELIVERED

DATE	SUBJECT	TEXT	PLACE DELIVERED	REMARKS

RECORD OF SERMONS DELIVERED

DATE	SUBJECT	TEXT	PLACE DELIVERED	REMARKS

RECORD OF SERMONS DELIVERED

DATE	SUBJECT	TEXT	PLACE DELIVERED	REMARKS

RECORD OF SERMONS DELIVERED

DATE	SUBJECT	TEXT	PLACE DELIVERED	REMARKS

RECORD OF SERMONS DELIVERED

DATE	SUBJECT	TEXT	PLACE DELIVERED	REMARKS

RECORD OF SERMONS DELIVERED

DATE	SUBJECT	TEXT	PLACE DELIVERED	REMARKS

RECORD OF SERMONS DELIVERED

DATE	SUBJECT	TEXT	PLACE DELIVERED	REMARKS

RECORD OF SERMONS DELIVERED

DATE	SUBJECT	TEXT	PLACE DELIVERED	REMARKS

RECORD OF SERMONS DELIVERED

DATE	SUBJECT	TEXT	PLACE DELIVERED	REMARKS

RECORD OF SERMONS DELIVERED

DATE	SUBJECT	TEXT	PLACE DELIVERED	REMARKS

RECORD OF SERMONS DELIVERED

DATE	SUBJECT	TEXT	PLACE DELIVERED	REMARKS

RECORD OF SERMONS DELIVERED

DATE	SUBJECT	TEXT	PLACE DELIVERED	REMARKS

RECORD OF SERMONS DELIVERED

DATE	SUBJECT	TEXT	PLACE DELIVERED	REMARKS

RECORD OF SERMONS DELIVERED

DATE	SUBJECT	TEXT	PLACE DELIVERED	REMARKS

RECORD OF SERMONS DELIVERED

DATE	SUBJECT	TEXT	PLACE DELIVERED	REMARKS

RECORD OF SERMONS DELIVERED

DATE	SUBJECT	TEXT	PLACE DELIVERED	REMARKS

RECORD OF SERMONS DELIVERED

DATE	SUBJECT	TEXT	PLACE DELIVERED	REMARKS

RECORD OF SERMONS DELIVERED

DATE	SUBJECT	TEXT	PLACE DELIVERED	REMARKS

RECORD OF SERMONS DELIVERED

DATE	SUBJECT	TEXT	PLACE DELIVERED	REMARKS

RECORD OF SERMONS DELIVERED

DATE	SUBJECT	TEXT	PLACE DELIVERED	REMARKS

RECORD OF SERMONS DELIVERED

DATE	SUBJECT	TEXT	PLACE DELIVERED	REMARKS

RECORD OF SERMONS DELIVERED

DATE	SUBJECT	TEXT	PLACE DELIVERED	REMARKS

RECORD OF SERMONS DELIVERED

DATE	SUBJECT	TEXT	PLACE DELIVERED	REMARKS

RECORD OF SERMONS DELIVERED

DATE	SUBJECT	TEXT	PLACE DELIVERED	REMARKS

RECORD OF SERMONS DELIVERED

DATE	SUBJECT	TEXT	PLACE DELIVERED	REMARKS

RECORD OF SERMONS DELIVERED

DATE	SUBJECT	TEXT	PLACE DELIVERED	REMARKS

RECORD OF SERMONS DELIVERED

DATE	SUBJECT	TEXT	PLACE DELIVERED	REMARKS

RECORD OF SERMONS DELIVERED

DATE	SUBJECT	TEXT	PLACE DELIVERED	REMARKS

RECORD OF SERMONS DELIVERED

DATE	SUBJECT	TEXT	PLACE DELIVERED	REMARKS

RECORD OF SERMONS DELIVERED

DATE	SUBJECT	TEXT	PLACE DELIVERED	REMARKS

RECORD OF SERMONS DELIVERED

DATE	SUBJECT	TEXT	PLACE DELIVERED	REMARKS

RECORD OF SERMONS DELIVERED

DATE	SUBJECT	TEXT	PLACE DELIVERED	REMARKS

RECORD OF SERMONS DELIVERED

DATE	SUBJECT	TEXT	PLACE DELIVERED	REMARKS

RECORD OF SERMONS DELIVERED

DATE	SUBJECT	TEXT	PLACE DELIVERED	REMARKS

RECORD OF SERMONS DELIVERED

DATE	SUBJECT	TEXT	PLACE DELIVERED	REMARKS

RECORD OF SERMONS DELIVERED

DATE	SUBJECT	TEXT	PLACE DELIVERED	REMARKS

RECORD OF SERMONS DELIVERED

DATE	SUBJECT	TEXT	PLACE DELIVERED	REMARKS

RECORD OF SERMONS DELIVERED

DATE	SUBJECT	TEXT	PLACE DELIVERED	REMARKS

RECORD OF SERMONS DELIVERED

DATE	SUBJECT	TEXT	PLACE DELIVERED	REMARKS

RECORD OF SERMONS DELIVERED

DATE	SUBJECT	TEXT	PLACE DELIVERED	REMARKS

RECORD OF SERMONS DELIVERED

DATE	SUBJECT	TEXT	PLACE DELIVERED	REMARKS

RECORD OF SERMONS DELIVERED

DATE	SUBJECT	TEXT	PLACE DELIVERED	REMARKS

RECORD OF SERMONS DELIVERED

DATE	SUBJECT	TEXT	PLACE DELIVERED	REMARKS

RECORD OF SERMONS DELIVERED

DATE	SUBJECT	TEXT	PLACE DELIVERED	REMARKS

RECORD OF SERMONS DELIVERED

DATE	SUBJECT	TEXT	PLACE DELIVERED	REMARKS

RECORD OF SERMONS DELIVERED

DATE	SUBJECT	TEXT	PLACE DELIVERED	REMARKS

RECORD OF SERMONS DELIVERED

DATE	SUBJECT	TEXT	PLACE DELIVERED	REMARKS

RECORD OF SERMONS DELIVERED

DATE	SUBJECT	TEXT	PLACE DELIVERED	REMARKS

RECORD OF SERMONS DELIVERED

DATE	SUBJECT	TEXT	PLACE DELIVERED	REMARKS

RECORD OF PASTORAL CALLS

YEAR	NAME OF CHURCH	NO. OF CALLS	YEAR	NAME OF CHURCH	NO. OF CALLS

RECORD OF EVANGELISTIC MEETINGS HELD

DATE	PLACE	LENGTH OF MEETING	NO. OF CONVER-SIONS	NUMBER RECLAIMED	NO. OF ACCESSIONS	REMARKS

RECORD OF EVANGELISTIC MEETINGS HELD

DATE	PLACE	LENGTH OF MEETING	NO. OF CONVER-SIONS	NUMBER RECLAIMED	NO. OF ACCESSIONS	REMARKS

RECORD OF EVANGELISTIC MEETINGS HELD

DATE	PLACE	LENGTH OF MEETING	NO. OF CONVER-SIONS	NUMBER RECLAIMED	NO. OF ACCESSIONS	REMARKS

RECORD OF SPECIAL FUNDS RAISED

DATE	CHURCH	QUOTA	AMOUNT RAISED	DEFICIT OR OVER-PAYMENT	REMARKS

RECORD OF CHURCHES BUILT

YEAR	PLACE	COST	SEATING CAPACITY	DEBT AFTER COMPLETION	DEDICATED BY

RECORD OF PARSONAGES BUILT

YEAR	PLACE	COST	NO. OF ROOMS	DEBT AFTER COMPLETION	REMARKS

RECORD OF LECTURES AND SPECIAL ADDRESSES DELIVERED

DATE	SUBJECT	PLACE	OCCASION	FEE	REMARKS

RECORD OF LECTURES AND SPECIAL ADDRESSES DELIVERED

DATE	SUBJECT	PLACE	OCCASION	FEE	REMARKS

RECORD OF LECTURES AND SPECIAL ADDRESSES DELIVERED

DATE	SUBJECT	PLACE	OCCASION	FEE	REMARKS

RECORD OF LECTURES AND SPECIAL ADDRESSES DELIVERED

DATE	SUBJECT	PLACE	OCCASION	FEE	REMARKS

RECORD OF LECTURES AND SPECIAL ADDRESSES DELIVERED

DATE	SUBJECT	PLACE	OCCASION	FEE	REMARKS

RECORD OF LECTURES AND SPECIAL ADDRESSES DELIVERED

DATE	SUBJECT	PLACE	OCCASION	FEE	REMARKS

RECORD OF LECTURES AND SPECIAL ADDRESSES DELIVERED

DATE	SUBJECT	PLACE	OCCASION	FEE	REMARKS

RECORD OF LECTURES AND SPECIAL ADDRESSES DELIVERED

DATE	SUBJECT	PLACE	OCCASION	FEE	REMARKS

RECORD OF WRITINGS PUBLISHED

DATE	TITLE	PUBLISHED BY	FEE	REMARKS

RECORD OF WRITINGS PUBLISHED

DATE	TITLE	PUBLISHED BY	FEE	REMARKS

RECORD OF WRITINGS PUBLISHED

DATE	TITLE	PUBLISHED BY	FEE	REMARKS

RECORD OF SALARY RECEIVED

YEAR	CHURCH	SALARY PROMISED		SALARY RECEIVED		HOUSE RENT		TOTAL SALARY RECEIVED	

RECORD OF SALARY RECEIVED

YEAR	CHURCH	SALARY PROMISED		SALARY RECEIVED		HOUSE RENT		TOTAL SALARY RECEIVED	

RECORD OF PERQUISITES RECEIVED ANNUALLY

YEAR	PLACE	FROM WEDDINGS	FROM FUNERALS	FROM OTHER SOURCES	TOTAL	REMARKS

RECORD OF PERQUISITES RECEIVED ANNUALLY

YEAR	PLACE	FROM WEDDINGS		FROM FUNERALS		FROM OTHER SOURCES		TOTAL		REMARKS

RECORD OF SPECIAL PERSONAL GIFTS RECEIVED

DATE	PLACE	GIVER	NATURE OF GIFT	OCCASION OF GIVING

RECORD OF SPECIAL PERSONAL GIFTS RECEIVED

DATE	PLACE	GIVER	NATURE OF GIFT	OCCASION OF GIVING

RECORD OF VACATION PERIODS

YEAR	LENGTH OF VACATION	WHERE SPENT	HOW SPENT	TOTAL EXPENSE		REMARKS

RECORD OF VACATION PERIODS

YEAR	LENGTH OF VACATION	WHERE SPENT	HOW SPENT	TOTAL EXPENSE		REMARKS

SUMMARIZED RECORD OF THE LIFE MINISTRY

YEAR	CHURCH	BAPTISMS	MEMBERS RECEIVED	MARRIAGES	FUNERALS	SERMONS DELIVERED	PASTORAL CALLS	SALARY	HOUSE RENT	PERQUISITES	TOTAL INCOME	REMARKS

SUMMARIZED RECORD OF THE LIFE MINISTRY

YEAR	CHURCH	BAPTISMS	MEMBERS RECEIVED	MARRIAGES	FUNERALS	SERMONS DELIVERED	PASTORAL CALLS	SALARY	HOUSE RENT	PERQUI-SITES	TOTAL INCOME	REMARKS

SUMMARIZED RECORD OF THE LIFE MINISTRY

YEAR	CHURCH	BAPTISMS	MEMBERS RECEIVED	MARRIAGES	FUNERALS	SERMONS DELIVERED	PASTORAL CALLS	SALARY	HOUSE RENT	PERQUI-SITES	TOTAL INCOME	REMARKS